NATURE'S TAPESTRY

Edited by

Rachael Radford

First published in Great Britain in 2002 by
POETRY NOW
Remus House,
Coltsfoot Drive,
Peterborough, PE2 9JX
Telephone (01733) 898101
Fax (01733) 313524

HB ISBN 0 75434 395 2
SB ISBN 0 75434 396 0

FOREWORD

Although we are a nation of poets we are accused of not reading poetry, or buying poetry books. After many years of listening to the incessant gripes of poetry publishers, I can only assume that the books they publish, in general, are books that most people do not want to read.

Poetry should not be obscure, introverted, and as cryptic as a crossword puzzle: it is the poet's duty to reach out and embrace the world.

The world owes the poet nothing and we should not be expected to dig and delve into a rambling discourse searching for some inner meaning.

The reason we write poetry (and almost all of us do) is because we want to communicate: an ideal; an idea; or a specific feeling. Poetry is as essential in communication, as a letter; a radio; a telephone, and the main criterion for selecting the poems in this anthology is very simple: they communicate.

CONTENTS

THE TREE OF LIFE

Have you seen a new-born palm
and felt its tight-formed flesh?
Leaves and stalk pre-packed with care
in best sequential mesh.

Have you watched its life unfurl
in geometric form?
The spreading radial fingers
in symmetry conform.

Up it thrusts, then slowly curves
with parabolic grace;
linear depth now soft'ning to
full circular embrace.

Sharp become its tender points -
soft innocence absconds;
corrugations of the trunk
mark graves of once hewn fronds.

Rustling wind, the bulbul's song,
a sheaf of blood-red dates;
ostrich-feathered duster plumes
await - at Allah's gates.

Edward Fursdon

PATCHWORK

Dusk, a patchwork quilt spread
over trees and meadows;
Warren, set, foxhole, well hid
from prying eyes;
Late birds on slight, misty wing
heading for the nest;
Walkers, ramblers, hastily
checking compasses;
Children at play looking out
for text messages;
Middle England, on the edge
of things temporal;
Green campaigners counting
hard-won laurels;
Curtain closing on one last peep
at a hazy beauty;
Tasting raw smells of earthiness
and buttermilk sky;
Empathy with a nightingale's
plea to be left in peace;
Random stars brought down,
like clay pigeons . . .
by bonfires in back gardens
always taking liberties;
Bats, alley cats, all putting a shine
on the Sandman's boot . . .
whose task to get us ready
for the next clay shoot;
World, coming together briefly
to try and patch us up.

R N Taber

FIDELITY

To feel her muscles under my thighs;
to feel her tresses in my eyes;
the musky sweetness of her scent
when hours of intimacy are spent
grooming, nuzzling, talking, feeling.
That's horse-sense.

Pearl Foy

THE LITTLE DEER

The sunlight played on her dappled coat
As she lay peacefully in the glade
And the sunbeams glinted through the trees
As her dreams began to fade

When she woke up with a frightened start
At the sound of the huntsman's horn
And the yelping hounds and horses' hooves
All running at the break of morn

The huntsmen in their scarlet coats
All pursuing the little deer
As she made one burst to get away
Her heart now frozen with fear

She saw her chance, she climbed the rocks
Her foot was swift and sure
Far below were the huntsmen now
The climb they could not endure

High up on the mountainside
The sun had started to set
And the little deer rested by the waterfall
And thought, my life's not over yet.

The sunlight played on her dappled coat
As she lay peacefully in the glade
And the last of the sunbeams glinted through the trees
As she took up her dreams in the shade.

Sharon Magennis

ENGLISH HERITAGE

It's grand country here,
In the greenest of the valleys
How beautiful they stand
All over the pleasant land.
Banner yellow, glorious golden,
Through shade and sunny gleam
The ruler of the realm was seen.

Up the top! Seeing the whirring town
The huffy smoke beaten down by black rain
A few bushes beat the funnelling winds,
Along the great world of England
Smiling over the silvery brooks,
With all the pearl and ruby glowing
Regard the magnificence of its heritage.

I grudgingly admitted this was true
So I come up to the top every day
To seek this bonny beauty,
Smelt the pleasant green pastures
While the bonny heart of the land
Is the English heritage packed with surprising gleam,
Home is where the heart is
And the English heritage around me.

Heather Aspinall

To A Daffodil

Daffodil, bright butterfly of spring,
How many times have I seen you dance
On fragile wing,
Across the landscape of my dream?
Bringing memories of some forgotten scene.

Sweet fragrance, tearing at the heart,
What thoughts you bring of days
That are long passed,
When age seemed just another point of view,
And youthful eyes saw everything as new.

Ah, harbinger of promise! Even now,
When dreams and hopes are scattered on the wind,
Your spirit reaches me, bringing forth fresh memory,
Of a long gone day,
And my mother's hand upon your delicate array.

Beryl L Lambert

SPRING CHILD

Heigh-ho!
I spy on yonder bank
a foundling child of spring;
pouting forth broad lustrous leaves
and sinuous probes with silken sheathes
enfolding fairy parasols,
pale yellow and petite.

High-ho!
She grows, sweet petals arched,
resplendent in the sun;
bright with hosts of tiny spheres,
of joy, sheer joy in growing wild,
a-quiver in the breeze.

And-oh!
The perfume of her breath,
of her pristine flowers:
primrose aptly takes her name,
though archly, without blush of shame
she tempts the bumblebee nearby
to kiss her shiny cheek.

John Maisey

WINTER CANVAS

Dawn breaks revealing white wonder
Spread wide for eyes to devour.
This no thick crisp blanket of snow
Piling high in every hedgerow.

Winter her first hoarfrost displays.
Nature wears her mantle of lace.
Jealous old queen guarding her jewel
Shimmering crystal oh so cruel.

Voices ring, clarity of bells
Breath freezes as it's expelled.
Fingers and toes numb, frost smitten
Mockery of the woollen mitten.

Twitching net curtains show parents
Watch offspring joyful and vibrant.
Large noisy seagulls screeching swoop,
Heading inland searching, they loop.

Sun beams an indulgent lover
Knowing he'll dispel her cover.
Brief beauty gone - canvas wiped clean
Nature waits to repaint the scene.

Kathleen Potter

BENEATH A POPLAR

Beneath a poplar is my solitude.
Leaves, which in my hand at first I clasp
I let fly, wind-blown, scattering on the grass.
And then the haze of autumn days has come
And the rich brown earth is revealed
By the plough blade.
The lombardy, mature, now sleeps in the glade,
For winter chill is drawing closely on;
And then the dry leaves curl,
And fringed by frost, their colour gone
To faded brown and then to skeletal grey,
Till snow will cover them with blanket white,
They disappear by spring and rot away
To join the soil from which they once derived.
And so the tree with nutrients is supplied.

Jon Lec

THE MIGHTY OAK

How I love the early morning dew on my leaves
My branches blowing softly in the breeze
The frosty mornings have gone, spring won't be long
I love the ash, elm, lime and the pine
The beautiful weeping willow, with its boughs that gently billow
Also the poplar and the beech, but my size they will never reach
For I am the largest in the land, so very tall I stand

Springtime has now arrived; the swallows swoop and dive
Owls perch and ravens search
The cold winds are stilled, now it's time to build
The tree creeper and blue tits nest
The purple emperor butterfly, on my leaves rest
The dormouse I also house
They all live in my hollows, all but the swallows

My boughs sway gently to the rhythm of the breeze
Slightly turning back my leaves
The warm sun on my bark, and a passing lark
It's that time of year; summer is here
With rabbits, hares and deer
Birds singing on a hot day, men working to bring in the hay

Now it's autumn and squirrels run
Up and down my branches with little dances
My fruit is the acorn, my leaves they adorn
The squirrel feeds and hordes for the winter it stores
Some they bury in the mud and wet, some they just forget
These will grow into a tree, big and mighty just like me
It's nearly time my leaves to shed, for they are becoming rather dead

Winter's here my leaves have now gone,
So have the birds and their song
The winds they now do blow, very strong high and low
Thunder and lightning storms, like the Devil with horns
But I am too big and strong, a branch or two my be gone
I have no fears, I can live for a 1000 years.

Barbara Gaetches

A Day In January

A very windy start to the day,
trees are in a swirling sway,
branches are buffeted by the strong, howling wind -
the sun emerges tentatively
through the moving spaces
created by the unceasing sway!
The momentary calm
    breathes
        silence.

Daphne F M

THE SNOWDROP

Strange that this so delicate of flowers
Should have such strength!
That its small drooping head
Pure white and lightly edged in palest green
Can push up through the frost-hard earth
- That it can brave strong winds and slashing rain
And bloom serene
Untouched
Unharmed
While still the tortoise hibernates
And dormouse sleeps in snug retreat!

Yet not so strange!
Many a human soul
Many fragile birds and flowers
Possess this steel-like inner core
This hardiness
This strength in seeming weakness
That appeals
    Inspires
        Uplifts
            Encourages!

Pate

THE FALLS

Niagara.
Slate-grey water
Hurls itself unceasingly
In solid masses
Over the horse-shoe edge
Into the foaming, boiling depths below.
Spray hangs in the sunlight,
Drifting like a curtain
Above the thundering water.
A rainbow
Curves above the brow of the gorge
Like a majestic coronet
Of multicoloured light.
The air is filled
With the incessant roar
Of the plunging, mighty falls.
Time seems suspended
As the senses are assailed
With such an immensity
Of sight and sound.

As for me,
I stand in silence,
Those beside me forgotten,
Made small and insignificant
By the awesome, unremitting power
Of God's creation.

Peter English

SOAKED IN MY PRAYING
(Will Spring Ever Come?)

I search over the deep green with hopeful optimism, but still see grey,
And wonder to myself whether this perpetual squall will cease.
For an age, but it feels so much longer, the earth has been sodden,
Along with urns and pots.
And the usually vivacious garden languidly leans, no longer
In alignment, a home for squatting debris.
How much more will it take before it gives up?
How much longer will Demeter be searching? We pray for her return,
And with her, her daughter.

I dream of the smell of verbena and naked feet perambulating
Through dry grass.
Please come home to us Persephone, and with you bring Shakespeare's
Hot eye of heaven to dry us all.
For along these borders this sunless green pleads for companionship,
Soaked in its praying, praying to give life,
Dampened in its grief, grieving for its unborn.
Come kneel with me Satyr and help save your home,
For I am but a neophyte in this new game you gods are playing.

Peter J McBride

THE EVENING ON THE CANAL

I would in an evening
Something be seen
Something seen and thought
Of beauty
As clouds fleeting by
In the evening sky
As mayflies are dancing
In the long grasses
A slight breeze
Blows my brow
The waters flow
Gently through
Where we have moored
All in all
By idyllic English countryside
A yellow light shines from within the boat
While faintly can be heard from inside
A stove boiling
The scene
Like the pages of a book turning
Of some story
Yet untold
As the light finally fades
Into the boat I will descend
The day remembered.

C J Bayless

MOMENTS

I fell in love
with that moment
of shared experience:
a heron preening
the ruffle of her feathers.
Then, taking wing,
arrow-fished and
broke the surface
    a slick of death remaining.

I fell in love
with that moment
your hand reached to mine
and, with knowing eye, winked
entry to a stranger.
This realm of love and
light wrought a trace
of wonderment
    to the child within.

I fell in love
with that moment
we drank the rain
as it fell,
as we walked without
regard. The brook
of words between us
told all there was
    to tell with no word spoken.

Michael Fenton

THE SKY

What a canvas the sky is.
An artist's brush cannot capture
The ever-changing hues and patterns.

Blues that differ in depth and colour,
Greys that merge into other greys,
And then there is wispy white or black.

Tumbling clouds above and below,
Fluffed up like velvet snow,
Light, dark, the whole spectrum covered.

There are oceans of layer upon layer,
Explosions of colours, pictures all there
With a mosaic of white showing through.

See the ripples of light floating past
As the sea seems to talk to the sky
And the clouds reflect back in reply.

There are rainbows that light up the sky
And whisper to the heart bringing joy
Making one want to dance, laugh and sing.

Sunset, sunrise, moon and sun,
Such magnificence shows a great hand.
A promise of other worlds, other life.

Stars twinkle like jewels in a velvet sky
And with the moon and sun guide and direct,
Sailor, explorer, traveller and tramper.

So as the moon directs the tide
We too are caught up in the web
Of learning from earth, sea and sky.

Our lives affected given deeper meaning
When we open our eyes to the beauty and wisdom
Seen with that glance at the sky.

Pamela Gillies

SHORT-SIGHTED

We take so much for granted and sometimes we don't see the flowers
that smell so sweet and the birds that sing tunefully.
Trees many different shades of green, some tall, some plump,
some wee, wild animals all around us, some have a huge family.
Countryside so peaceful, real tranquillity, a haven for town people
who live in the city.

Bees a'buzzing as they flit from flower to flower,
they never seem to run out of steam, seem to have much power.
Fields that go on for miles many lush and green with picturesque
houses dotted here and there in keeping with the scene.
We should appreciate our countryside, regularly watch
and keep it clean, because maybe when we're not looking
what is now will be has-been.

Sue Koert

THOUGHTS OF A BULRUSH

Long ago our roots would lay in pristine waters,
Wherever water-life existed,
Waterfowl were discreet, in weaving their nests at our feet,
Geese and mallards would stay, and bear their young,
For we the bulrush, would shelter them from the winds, rain and sun,

Frogs would spawn from which tadpoles would wriggle,
With young minnows darting here and there
And turtles basking in the sun,
Occasionally, a horse drawn jaunting cart would pass by,
Leaving the water-life undisturbed,
Now high-powered vehicles fly by, leaving deadly gases
                    which we absorb, and will eventually die,

Now stunted in growth we carry on,
But very soon we will be gone,
Then only on canvas will we be seen,
By human beings yet unborn,
Human beings must re-think, before they,
With everything else, become extinct,

Ecological preservation must be derived,
                    if our planet is to survive.

Albert V Hale

ALL THINGS UGLY AND FAT

All things bright and beautiful
All things ugly and fat,
The vampire bat
A long toothed rat
Can you see the beauty in that?

Plod, times one hundred, a wriggling centipede,
Hiss and slither, get that snake away from me.
A cockroach feeding,
A soldier ant leading
Where's the beauty? Why it's gleaming.

He glides along
He scuttles so fast
He waves in motion
Side to front to back.
He collects with precision
He gathers his load.
All things bright and beautiful
Whether ugly, fat or old.

Susan Sissons

OH GREEN LEAF!

Oh green leaf! Now you've turned brown
Where do you roam
Are you on your way home?
As that branch lets you go
You meander on down
Look at the sights, the sights all around
The village, the hills, trees
Are all there to be seen
As they double in size from where you have been
Floating on air
Dodging the crowd
It's quiet on top, the bottom is loud.
Oh green leaf, now you've turned brown
Where do you roam?
Gently sifting the ground
You've found your way home.

Steve Randell

MILFORD SOUNDS

You call me and I don't
know why -
Milford sounds
sounds of babies
and confusion and you.

In fact the lake is
peaceful
cloaked with mallard
and his mate.
Black long-necked swans -
and Japanese pretending
to catch carp
with graphite fishing rods.
When I saw a shining,
vibrant, sparkling
rainbow trout
lifted.

Sail boats flap around
the dead man's body
in the lake.
Nearby in the quarry
my soul-mate
declares he swam there
dived from the cliff

and hurled himself
up a rope
to dive once more.

Two children playing
near the lakes
pretty girls

happily running, snapping twigs
brushing their hands against shrubs and
flowers
yet Milford sounds -
it's you
you need me
and I'm there - here
and so is your new baby.

Christina C Simpson

THE DAWNING

Dark, diamond dusk
Hugging the night,
And blowing out the light,
From inside star-studded skies.

Dawn lonely waits
Lulling night awake
Into a paler
Shade of sky.

Blue topaz and sapphires,
Lighting the sky,
With diamonds on fire,
Making our hearts sigh
On this scene of delight.

The clouds rise
Like sleeping eyes
As dawn darkly shines,
Inside the shade of time,
And the waking - sunrise, sighs.

Shirley Kelleher

THE SWAN KING

The chorus rings softly
His desire his dance
Towering up high within magical trance
Silky members proceed to flow
Across the plane of darkened glow
Dimming lights, flashing blades
Ballet dancing masquerades
Mystery and laughter rings golden bells
Bursting thereafter on which mentors dwells
Swirls and twirls from little girls
Shimmer costumes fancy pearls
Tiptoe softly, bouncing high
Pirouettes across the sky
Fly like a seagull, glide like a swan
Close down the curtains the opera has gone.

Lisa-Cresswell Wilkinson

THE BIRDS

The sun has fallen and they are gone -
The nightingale, swallow and swift,
But the red breasts together sing on,
Generous winter's conciliatory gift.

Enjoying Boreas' icy weather,
Friendly sparrows flit about the hedge,
Proving it's a vain endeavour
Standing still on rocky ledge.

Rivers and streams lie still and frozen,
Mini-glaciers throughout the land,
And yet one heron, his vigil unbroken,
Continues by the shore to stand.

Seagull and mallard, delights to see,
Skate supreme on thick-set ice,
Slipping and sliding, skidding free,
The frozen lake their paradise.

Foraging for a few scraps of food
The starlings whistle and console,
On snowy rooftops, deep, inbrued,
They slur and chuckle rigmarole.

Bogs swallow fallen trees,
The blizzard's violent aftermath,
And red grouse fly in ecstasies,
Throwing voices for a laugh.

And off the trees long icicles
And on the hills drifting snow,
In the wood an owl belittles
A Borean gale itching below.

In the winter as in the spring
Stonechat and chaffinch bring me joy,
Their song a strangely mythic thing:
Sirens, nymphs who exalt and buoy.

Heys Stuart Wolfenden

THE LIFE OF A CLOUD

Droplets of water that's vaporised
Rising to the sky, a cloud is born
Small and white, fluffy and wispy
Gathering droplets through the day
Now a cloud powerful, immense, gigantic

Sailing on the morning air
This way and that, some shelter for you
It gazes down upon the earth
Wind blowing it across the skies
My goodness, look ahead, tragedy

A mountain range is in your path
More clouds gather, you turn to grey
Wind buffeting you this way and that
Lightning strikes, thunder is heard
You rumble and grumble, there's nowhere to go

At last you are free, your droplets of water turned to rain
You climb out of the valley, skimming the mountain top
Behind alas are rivers deep, churning through the gorge
But wait, there are green shoots spouting
The valley turns to green, flowers bloom, birds sing a tune

Life giving water rejuvenating, others now find life
The sun shines down, the earth breathes again
All because a cloud was born, a long, long way away
Next time you see that cloud go past
Spare a thought for nature's rebirth.

Carole A Cleverdon

POISONED IVY

(The elephant is the only animal
that shares our ability to shed a tear of grief)

From years past she remembers still
that it was her he meant to kill;
how in her rage she chased the man,
who scorched the road with his van.

She stands alone. She sheds a tear
for her lost son she held so dear,
killed to profit those who tart
their bodies in the name of art.

Kings and queens of stately chess,
ivory tokens, valueless,
compared with animals that cry
recalling grief as years go by.
How remiss that miscreant man
can't enforce the ivory ban.

Peter Huggins

WALKING THE DOG

Walking -
Healthy and invigorating exercise
For dog and owner both,
Leaving the mind free to roam at will.

Green fields and hills
And cottage gardens rioting with flowers,
The natural beauties of the world
Bring calm and peace to troubled mind,
A setting down of burdens,
A lifting of the spirits
As the birds soar high above me in the sky.

Pausing to gaze around,
Hidden beauties are revealed:
Tiny petals nestling in the hedgerows,
Insects humming busily in bell-shaped flowers.

The dog finds new exciting scents,
Pauses, extracting much delight,
And then moves on.
I follow her,
Eager for new and unexpected sights,
Scenes and experiences all fresh.
Winding lanes and paths
That keep their secrets
Till, a corner turned,
Another natural wonder
Assails my senses,
Each of them alive,
Receptive
To sweet nature's charms.
Walkies!

Yes, please I
Anticipated daily joy!

Roma Davies

NATURAL ROUTINE

Tweet-tweet from the bush to the tree
Rustle-rustle
Jingle of the washing line
Nick a twig or three
Developing-constructing
That's safe and deep

Then it was eaten alive
In the summer cold breeze
The cats in the trees - fox, rats whatever
Vicious - ugly
This is our season of C = D = S
With piercing pressure on the world
C = D = S (if you're wondering)
Cold sores - dripping wet - a little *sun* (if you're *lucky*).

E A Triggs

NATURE'S BEAUTY

The white frothy waves gently breaking on the sand
The beach train goes lazily by
And the sea breeze is warmly fanned
Silver winged seagulls glide without a care
In a blue cloudless sky
And swoop to catch their fare
A rainbow, like a jewelled dome
Came to look and then went home
Waves dancing in the sunlight
A shimmering sapphire sea
Summer at its height
Unlocked by nature's key.

The rugged rocks across the bay
Stand in tall majestic splendour
King of all they survey
Home to a mixture of flowers and shrubs
Dotted about in colourful careless bouquet
The rocks their parasol hoods
Brightly winged butterflies pay their respects
And add to its beauty
Bees call for pollen to collect
Then fly away having done their duty

Nature's beauty is unique
To view, but not to own
We, only caretakers, so to speak
For nature we cannot clone
Embrace it to the full
It is here to stay
Unless its beauty we cull
And let it all decay.

June Egan

INVISIBLE SILK

This winter coat of invisible silk
Left on a chair turned inside out.
Touching bare skin, her silent skill
Remains of memories the ice cube chill.
Shall we like stray stars catch a glimpse?
Of a boiling sun frozen at the core,
Marvel at the beauty yet know not why
Believing like the truth there's purity there.
Are we so tranquil we blend without knowing?
Like the artist's smudges from his charcoal thumb.

Paul Willis

WINTER

You draw the curtains on a December morn
And your eyes are full of wonder
At the beauty of the dawn.
Not spring, or sunshine, fills you with delight.
But the blackness of a coalmine
At first is in your sight.
Dreary, dreary days of winter
Is your first dismal thought,
When on the horizon, enraptured
You are caught in the burning shades of red
That suddenly appear
From nowhere it would seem
As if from something dead
From yesterday you've fled.

You linger for a little while
As shapes begin to form,
A house, a silhouette of trees
And a church is born
Vision upon vision come gradually into view
A bird soars high above you
Fighting sleep and shaking off the dew,
Calling to all to see the beauty of the dawn.

P M Burton

PEACEFUL NIGHTLY WALKERS

A silent night,
Cool, misty air
On this, this summer's day.
Stars aiding visibility,
Misty residue of vapour
Lingering over the
Aroma of scented flowers
Like a momentous longing,
Calling of care
And arms embracing
Thus nightly walkers
Ending, this, this beautiful
Evening of a summer's day.

R Whisko

SUMMER

We wake to a beautiful sunrise
Birds sing a chorus at dawn
The winds caress, the earth is blest
Then surely summer is born

Flowers in the meadows, sheep on the hill
Red poppies appear in the corn
When trees are laden with blossom
Then surely summer is born

Rainbows arched across the sky
Dewdrops on roses each morn
Trees are dressed in their Sunday best
Then surely summer is born

When leaves are falling like raindrops
Their beauty all tattered and torn
We see mist on yonder mountains
Then surely summer has gone.

Lydia Barnett

SUMMER

Summer warm
Summer hot
Summer blazing
Through windows
Summer precious
With hope
Summer, beautiful summer,
Is here to shine
Upon you.

C A Keohane

SUMMER BLACKBIRD

Black of plume, divine in song
summer blackbird stay with me,
evening joy to hear always
yet winter comes and joy is gone.

Shadows now and you and I meet
on chilled garden earth,
mourn together summer's gone but
brightly shines your golden eye.

Mute your voice in dark December
yet sleeps there in the earth below
seeds of summer joy and song -
remember. Oh remember!

Michael Rowson

WINDY DAY

Wind, curving through the neighbourhood
Fast over the hard concrete, treacherous
For the clinging child, enveloping the luxuriant hydrangeas
Always round the ginnels and gaps in the fence
Watch closely, the abundance of the contemplative wind.

M Courtney Soper

ONE SUMMER'S DAY

Dawn's first pale streak that ushers in the day that is to be,
Soft, velvet-petalled roses, damp with early morning dew;
A thousand sparkling diamonds dancing on a sunlit sea
That breaks on shell-strewn sands; a sky of azure blue.

Dog roses in the hedgerows, forget-me-nots by the rill,
The scent of creamy meadowsweet and wains of new-mown hay;
Leaves whispering in the wind, blithe birds' melodious trill,
The joyful calls and laughter of children at their play.

A picnic in the woods, 'mid foxgloves and humming bees,
A wedding in the village, a white-robed, blushing bride,
Attended by infant flower-girls, with posies of sweet peas,
Glides slowly down the aisle, at her smiling father's side.

The church clock chimes the passing hours, the day,
                         though long, must close,
A glittering pathway guilds the sea, the sun sinks ever lower,
A sky of egg-shell blue, and clouds suffused with gold and rose,
Bid a glorious farewell! One summer's day is o'er.

Muriel Willa

SPRING SYMPHONY

Catkins blow on hazel twigs
along the woodland ride.
Celandines and primroses
freckle the countryside.
Perched on a thickset hawthorn
a glossy blackbird sings
a loud sweet song
in praise of God.
Creator of the spring.

Rooks wheel and caw -
a raucous sound -
above the tallest trees.
Black-feathered rags
tossed too and fro
on the equinoctial breeze.
Bright butterflies, fat bumbling bees
and nesting birds that sing,
unite in praise,
give thanks to God,
Creator of the spring.

Small flittermice,
soft-feathered owls,
all creatures great and small
join in the glorious song of praise
to God,
who made us all.

Jess Chambers

JUNE

The field of rye is singing sibilantly soft,
The warm west wind is bringing sweet scents from meadow croft
Where the piled hay
Perfumes the day,
And the cuckoo fluteth oft.

The patterned brake is springing delicately curled
Where the honeysuckle's clinging nectar horns are whirled,
And the dear wild rose
In the dark hedge glows,
And the daisies crown is pearled.

Now is the year desirable and duly wooed,
The dappled treetops tell her grace, she is pursued;
Tender is she
To breeze and bee,
And she yields with fragrance her maidenhood.

Joyce Barton

SNOWY SPRINGTIME DAWN

The silence is serene,
For the snow has not been seen.
Except by me.

The birds one by one all awaken,
The silence is suddenly broken.
I listen.

My mind a mass of emotion,
The sunrise on the horizon.
I stand still, and watch, and listen.

I know the snow must mean it is cold,
But I feel wonderfully warm.
Peace to think, peace to feel;

This snowy springtime dawn.

Joleen Kuyper

A MOONLIGHT SURF IN SUMMER
(For Mike)

He came swiftly
Sweeping through the crests
Riding the highest and the best
Letting it take him
Strongly into the shallows
The moonlight flickering
Making white and gold patches
On the moving sea
Coolness of the summer late evening
Becoming
A balm upon the spirit
An inner sense
To pursue pleasure
And ease the stress
Bringing an uplifting sensation
From the highest and the best.

Anne Veronica Tisley

AN ODE TO SUMMER

Deep in greenwood glades I stroll
Where nodding bluebells kiss the air
Of scented summer. Oaken boughs
Spread their broad-leaved canopy
As carolling birds, with accents pure,
Sing sweet odes of festal joy;
A thousand dancing shadows play
In silent melody as shafts
Of sunlight slant in golden beams
Through trellis-works of foliage.

I find my favourite oak, and lie
Beneath its shade, refreshed and cool;
And through the ever-shifting motley
Traced by latticed boughs and branches
Glints of patterned sunshine glance
In rainbow colours manifold -
A bright kaleidoscope of hues
As mottled as a fine mosaic.

Dreams of summer steal upon me;
And I doze in verdant realms
Until a distant song arises
Deep within my heart of hearts,
Yet from within the woods themselves.
I rise unbidden from my couch
And follow, in a trance, that sound
Whose murmur, I now realise,
Has lingered with me all along.
For there, beyond a fragrant greensward,
Wells the purest fountain spring -
A crystal stream whose harmonies
Echo those of Heaven itself.

Robert D Hayward

SUMMER GARDEN

My senses are alerted
as youth meets maturity
and delicate but daring spring
blossoms to beauteous summer,
rearranging nature's tapestry.
Above, the bluest sky,
emblazoned by golden sunshine;
beneath, the greenest grass,
festooned with flowers, shrubs and trees,
a kaleidoscopic paint-box of delight.
A central glittering coronet
catches the light from every angle
as it tumbles and ripples across the pond
where peaceful fish swim.
I close my eyes and listen.
The sound of the water soothes,
the birds sing their perfect song
and a distant buzz announces
the arrival of a busy bumblebee.
A gentle breeze rustles the leaves
and sways the flowers in unison. Their
perfume is intoxicating and mingles
with the mossy waft of mown grass.
Breathing in I fill my lungs
with air so fresh it makes me dizzy.
The warmth of the sun entices
me to rest, and the soft breeze
returns to refresh me.

Such complete bliss!
An English garden on a summer's day.

Julie Holness

A WALK BY THE RIVER

September
and along the river bank
Himalayan Balsam flaunts
pink and purple petticoats.

A heron hunched and still
suddenly wheels, brilliant wing
out of sunlight rising.

The landscape in a green drowning
surrenders boundaries and lines
to clambering grass and nettles.

Submerged, patient,
it waits for change
and winter's stark sculpting,

When tree silhouettes sharpen,
dark rocks shape the skyline,
fields are revealed, hedgerows sparkle.

The landscape breathes again.

Alice Rawlinson

SUMMER AFTERNOON

The climbing rose is flushed
    with warm, scented blossom
        which charms the nose.

The cascade chatters and chuckles
    its way into the pool,
        where golden fish
laze under round, green pads
    which are a platform
        for a burst of colour.

Garden furniture is set for tea.
    Female feet shed their shoes
        then sink with gratitude
            into soft, cool lawn.

Cups of tea – and cakes
    from the morning toil -
        prompt welcome nods of appreciation

Gracious living!

Nothing disturbs the summer afternoon
    until - a wasp -
hovers near the jam-filled sponge!

Kinsman Clive

ONE GREY DAY IN SPRING

The weather struck:
a brittle frost
in spring that stripped an elm tree bare
snuffing out at trifling cost
our vernal faith
that tragic year.

Shed was the elm's mantle
her trampled leaves
among the bracken fallen by her trunk
when the trashed foliage fell in sheaves
tipped with yellow
dry and shrunk.

Nature's was a hollow love
that spring to bestow
hollow like the elm so limp and broken
that scarce had time patiently to grow
stout branches
in spring's token.

Sad spring took
the poor elm's bounty
drained her dry, an elm in blossom
maimed one grey day in Kent county
as the battered tree struggled
in a maelstrom.

A crow cast her jaundiced eye about
helpless in the snow.
If only she could raise a shout
to curb spring's tale of woe.

Angus Richmond

HERE COMES THE SUN

Here comes the sun, a zest of life, it's a season we all wait for, as no one likes the cold winter weather as it gives them a chill, or wearing many clothes. So when the sun comes, everyone springs out with joy as they feel good, so they can walk bare, without any care in the world. The flowers and bees go together, as the sun wakes them up for any outing as the weather is a season of change, with all walks of life to face. Here comes the sun at last as the flowers bloom with different colours. The sun, full of light, comes from above. The sun wakes them to do lots of things, like the sea, which is close to nature, which is pure and innocent and free. Here comes the sun which is natural, where there is no charge as it is a gift from above. It warms you up and if you feel hot, a shade is a safe option. Everyone loves the sun as it brightens them up. Winter becomes a problem for many, as a lot of people don't like the cold. They also go to other places to get warm, as they don't get enough sun. So when the sun comes, they change with joy, as the sun gives them a zest for life. The sun has a lot of goodness which we take for granted. The days feel longer when there is a bag of sunshine to cheer them, as the weather becomes a major problem for all.

The weather gives them a zest for life as the sun is a gift of life.

F Jackson

WINTER

When cobwebs
Covered with silver dew fill the icy air,
Winter opens her shimmering coat and begins the day.

Icicles sharpen their knives
And cover the ground in a sheet of steel.
Flowers hide their heads in bed of earth,
Waiting for the sun's return.

Swirling mists of morning air
Coat the grass.
Sparkling diamond frost
Crowns the trees.

Light blankets of snowflakes
Run fingers of blue
Over things asleep,
Awaiting spring's sunlight.

Changeling elves dance
On pointed toes,
Tiptoeing over
Rivers of dragon scales.

Winter awakes,
She spreads her gown of white.
Mother Nature
Bows her head.

Michelle Baines

AUTUMN'S VOICE

darkness is a hidden sound
as the wind blows through
a tattered tree
a leaf falls into the mind's eye
golden memories of summer life
warmed by fire in dark cold nights
mystery is here in the rain
almost touchable before it escapes
sliding into wet ground
under magic moonrays old
touching shadows again
lives fall from the sky
that feel dark and alone
the sun does not shine
on the swaying treetops
blue torrents wash the heart
catch me I am falling
whispers the rain to a leaf
hold me in your tender hands
a crisp golden memory
that never hit the ground

J Ball

TEARS

Dawn . . .

I walk through the forest alone . . . though not really alone,
The songs for the birds, they accompany me.

I walk among the trees and look up at the weird and
Wonderful shapes of the clouds.

But there! There's one! Shaped just like a mushroom.

My eyes close as the rain from that cloud touched my cheeks.

It appears that same cloud is crying . . .

. . . Or could it be me?

John Reali

THE STEVENSON LIGHTS

A boat skidding through,
quixotic in the thrash of rain,
a tide climaxing at night:
those for whom the sea is element
salt and tough.

Fog. Hail. Faint sun.
Back and forth across a tract
of shallow sea, a marathon of months
or years on end, to win the Flannan,
Kintyre, Duncansby Head.

Reconnoitring surf, exploitation
of the day for all its worth -
they find an edge, managing
colliding winds and tides
to maximum advantage. See what

confidence in engineering they hand
each other, as if
they smell their way through shoal water,
dunes, estuaries, the deepest treacheries of the ocean
looking to undo them.

But seasons turn. The surface smoothes,
lifts itself to breathe
the scents of summer cliffs and men
make shift to infiltrate the sea. They build

and learn - tireless as gulls
locked into survival,
until a guardian band of lights,
as pickets round a sleeping army,
stands to: Bell Rock and May,
the Rhinns of Islay -
immaculate Skerryvore.

Josephine Brogan

NATURE

What a wonderful thing
Sight can be
When focused on the world we see
That natural beauty
That's before your eyes
Forever changing
As seasons go by
New growth, new life
It sprouts to the light
And blossoms and flourishes
As long days go by
It's all around you
No place untouched
There's beauty everywhere
All you have to do, is look
Freedom to live
To grow as it chooses
No interference
No man-made places
It's Mother Nature
At her very best
No bricks, no mortar
Just a haven of nests
Walk through it and absorb
Embrace it and behold
This beautiful world we live in
Is yours . . .

Christine A Walker

NATURE'S JEWELS

Winter wears her diamonds
In frost and whitest snow.
They gleam and flash and sparkle
The sunshine makes them so.
Spring wears lots of emeralds
On new-leafed bush and tree.
With amethysts of violets
Shows her fairest jewellery.
Summer wears a coronet
With buttercups of gold
And roses red as rubies
Most lovely to behold.
Autumn has her amber
With necklace pearls of dew
And bracelets made of berries
Of ash, hawthorn and yew.
Yes Nature has her jewellery
All seasons of the year
Have lots of gems to show us
As each of them appear.

Margaret B Baguley

ENGLAND OUR ENGLAND

Through feathered clouds I proudly look
See your patterned quilt a-glowing on the ground.
Intricately made, admired by all - this woven covering of fertile soil.
Your browns and greens make colourful patches.
Those shiny jewels are rows of houses, spiky turret erect and tall
And as the power of jets ascending, quilted patterns revealed to all.

More beds of fluffy feathers seem motionless, but still in flight we soar
Palest blue meets brightest white.
Is there a break in ozone layer?
Are we riding on a wing and a prayer?
Down through the clouds the shoreline's seen.

Snow-covered plains but not a soul in sight.
What I fear may be an imagery plight.
Rumpled tufts appear, could it be that children played there?
Snow's a-melting now, but is it really so - water can be seen,
                                                    way below
Trickling streams are now a-forming, down the glades, this
                                                    melted snow.

Lakes and streams are now adjoining.
Snow's now disappearing, like butter melting on fresh-baked dough
Span of water's getting wider, I am 'wandering slowly as a cloud . . .'
Who is there to share this with me: tingle in the heart, this lovely glow?
Banks of snow are now appearing, who's been shovelling in the night?
Bright light, white light, daylight, modern paintings in the sky
Of fluffy clouds that are too shy.

Look way down there, see cloth of sheerest voile
Further on see tulle with blobs of pointed cream.
Rough roads are coming up, bumps and dips are strongly felt
Turbulence is forecast. 'Fasten seatbelts!'
Fear in me I'm getting thirsty but not a hostess in sight.
We are gliding very smoothly, new roads are felt beneath the wheels.
Feet outstretched and I am comfy in this, upgraded space.

A C Yap-Morris

WIND, RAIN AND SUN

Wind reaps its restless harvest
As it passes by:
Rain, gently or heavy, makes manifest
Its healthful properties:
Sun sails majestically on course
In the quiescent sky:
And Earth always rejoices when in force
Are the influences of these natural deities.

Wind may be movement of air,
But it's its freedom we cannot ignore.
Rain may be precipitation from moist air,
But it's its cleansing touch that we adore.
Sun may be a star beyond protective air,
But it's its vital beneficence we revere.
And, being of Earth, we cannot do other than love
All three as nature directs us.

Were we made of less spirit and soul,
Then, maybe, we'd never regard them
As other than factual phenomena -
But wind, rain and sun bind us to them.

S V Batten

SUMMER IN CAMBRIDGE - JULY 1998
QUEEN'S COLLEGE GARDENS

The cold wind sweeps across the green
tormenting the leaf-bound trees
while young and old, the quiet and bold
fight the contentious breeze.
Around the green the abandoned cars
are left at owner's risk
on payment of an appropriate fee -
doing nothing to encourage thrift.
There is a bench on which I sit
and not another nigh.
I feel if I can brave the cold
by sitting in this spot
I shall die a death,
a wintry death,
in Cambridge in July!
So then I leave
the empty bench
to winter's stormy blast
and depart the scene
with words obscene
and heart by no means wrenched!

Andrew A Duncan

OUR SURROUNDING WORLD

As I lie, I feel the smooth texture of
Sand between my fingers and toes.
As I look up I see the sun
Going down and the night falling upon me.
I smell a sweet scent.

As I lie, I feel the smooth texture of
Sand between by finger and toes.
A look to my left I see the waves
Bashing against the cliff side
I smell a disturbing scent.

As I lie, I feel the smooth texture of
Sand between my fingers and toes
As I look to my right I see the emptiness
Of the green, green grass disappearing
I smell a wonderful scent.

As I lie, I feel the smooth texture of
Sand between my fingers and toes.
As I look up I see the rocks
So wild they make my eyes shine
I smell a dangerous scent.

Kayleigh Jones

IN PRAISE OF DAFFODILS

Humble, modest daffodil
In a jam jar on my sill,
You need no cut glass vase
To fill my room with joyful splendour.

How you brighten up the place
I'm glad to see your sunny face.
Outside the door, still winter's chill,
And yet here's springtime on my sill.

Anita Burgess

WIND

The fickle, the feckless, the frolicsome wind
Batters and blows on a chill autumn day
He rattles and rollicks some empty beer cans
They clatter and chatter along the highway.

Wind whistles down chimneys and skims over eaves
He fusses and flounces the autumn leaves
Red, gold and amber all prettily prance
They flirt and they flutter to join in the dance.

Wind batters and bellows, he rants and he rails
He pumps up some paper and skyward it sails
A plastic bag catches on wires overhead
No longer a bag, but a wind-sock instead.

Chins search for collars, and fingers go fumbling
Wind whistles wild, but not many are grumbling
Hats blow from heads, and skirts go all skittish
We don't complain? No, of course not - we're British.

Win Price

WALTZ OF THE CLOUDS

Dancers on a journey,
Across the open expanse of sky,
Chameleons,
Ever changing shape and colour,
Billowing,
Drifting randomly,
Water droplets suspended on high,
In a liaison with the atmosphere,
Galloping across the cobalt blue sky,
Towards some unknown destination,

White giants of wisped cotton wool curls,
Dancers in a variety of costumes,
Appearing in the arena above,
Taking to the stage,
When conditions dictate,
Some glide along,
Translucent veils wandering,
Others prance,
As if frisky groups of white ponies,
With wind-blown manes and swishing tails,

Floating feathers in formation move,
And across the canopy,
Voile seems draped, its ragged edges trailing,
Tufts of pink candyfloss wander at random,
A sorcerer soars with a cauldron steaming,
Its magic distributing,
Stratus,
Cirrus,
Cumulus,
Dancing in the waltz of the clouds.

Ann G Wallace

PAINTING WITH THE SKY

I look up at the sky and it reminds me of a painter's palette
The colours so bright and vivid

I want to touch the sky with my finger and mix all the colours together
Creating my own picture

But the clouds close in and the colours disappear
Like a painter putting down his brush
Inspiration fades away . . .

Carol Moore

THE SPIDER'S WEB

The spider's web is a wondrous sight
Woven carefully overnight
Fixed, glued and held in space
'Twixt twig and leaf
This minute trace
Exact and fine
Of gossamer line
Waiting - ready by morning time.

When comes the dawn
A perfect shape
With diamond dewdrops
Lies in wait
The trap is set for all to see
A lace of silver filigree.

It must be said, it's only fair
The spider's web is a deadly lair!

Mike Pannell

THE WIND

How can an invisible force uproot a tree?
How can a yacht be pushed cross the sea?
Where does it come from?
Where does it go?
This tremendous force
That the eye cannot see.

From where does it obtain its fuel
To drive it forward with such vengeance?
Why such destruction
Of all in its path?
Can't it be more gentle?
This unseen element.

Is man the perpetrator?
With progress untamed
Inventing new chemicals
In the name of vanity and wealth.
Destroying the atmosphere,
Thus giving rise to the *wind!*

Annette Murphy

THE LEOPARD

I sit in dappled sunlight that filters through the trees
As still as a statue, no more sound than the breeze
When I hunt I am a shadow, a silent plume of smoke
A phantom of the forest, a stalking, hunting ghost

Antelope, impala, gazelle and topi
Even a zebra is not too large for me
You're not aware when I am there
Though I'm watching just the same
I'm a master of my surroundings as I play the waiting game

With move and counter-move I creep through the grass
My prey strain all their senses to discover what I mask
Clever at concealment, evolution made me this way
My body bends with the grass, my tail a counter-weight

I hunt by sound and sight and scent
And step with silent paws, leap from tree to tree
And grasp prey with vice-like jaws
In daylight I am deadly but the night's my special friend
I can kill in a second and bring life to a tragic end

You human kind will see of me only a seldom glimpse
Though the machines you use destroy my habitat
I remain a constant presence, an elusive spotted cat.

David Horan

THE WAVE

Towards the shore
It glides
Slowly swelling
Gaining force
Arching itself
Ready for the plunge
Then, crashing down
Surges forward
Slipping back again
Ready for its encore.

Jane Richardson

HEARTBEAT

Deep in the heart of
the mountain tall.
Heard, as the forest tree will fall,
throughout this land of hill and glen,
beats the heart of freedom again.
Hear it echo in the straths,
within the capercaillies' call,
see it in the salmons' river leap,
the heartbeat within us all.
Shaking the stillness of waters deep,
waking them from slumber and sleep,
crying out in birthing pain,
a roar to free this land again.
Deep it lies in Celtic heart,
a thrumming thread of ancient tune,
that speaks of love torn apart,
by the pursuit of material gain.
In the air of mountain breeze,
lilting through the forest trees,
a song of redemption and release,
awaken again the ancient ways.

Andrew P McIntyre

NOTE THE ANGLE SUBTENDED

Lunar, seen from the mountain, a unique and threatening world
Like an overripe, decayed fruit,
Focus on the sky, and signs of intelligence
Yet lunar, with that fixed and metric size, though old
Is foursquare glowing with the sun . . . odd . . .

M C Soper

WINTER

When Master sits
And Mistress writes
And autumn tints the air
And winter steals away the light
And summer-scented fare
When fire burns upon the hearth
And logs spit sparks that fly
And happy voices rise and fall
As darkness fills the sky
When lamps are lit and cast their glow
On faces old and new
And candlelight makes shadows dance
Upon the parlour wall
When chimneys rattle on lofty height
As north wind wildly blows
And swinging gate on rusty hinge
Back and forward goes
When Jack Frost settles unannounced
And spreads his mantle wide
Over hawthorn and the briar
And takes all in his stride
When fire dies and eyes droop low
And tired voices wane
And ticking clock says time for bed
As the day draws to its close
And soon the house in silence lies
Asleep in deep repose.

EB

RAINBOW

The rain shone . . . the sun wept.
Glistening shafts of polished light
streamed down from silver clouds;
golden tears rolled from his face
and dripped their beaming drops to Earth.
Goddess-wise and witness to
their magic, she gave sanctuary
for their union . . .

. . . and tenderly, the rainlight kissed
the sunfall Seven times,
to bless and crown her patient heart
in Light's ethereal smile.

Christala Rosina

THE DAFFODIL

Upon an earthen bed fresh with moist and dew,
a little rain with no frost,
we all saw in a glorious mode the magic and life
of the natural symbolism as one life
lived in unity and harmony, blessing the eye
as we embraced the kings and queens who
cohabited a bed around the trees.
In the valleys lay the swans of symbiotic eugenics.

Madam Daffodil looked upon the sun
resplendent in all fired completeness,
Lord butterfly alighted upon a natural beauty.
She was the fairest and richest in colour.
A bee joined the mellifluous ensemble.
The wind stirred, the butterfly flew off
but like all nature, no unnatural genetics is employed.

Lady Daffodil had a moist centre.
The bee dived in humming as he went
creating a unique genesis,
order and peace reigned in the field.
The lily spoke to the daffodil.
The rose beautifully intoned but the
buttercup was to milk all the glory.
When the day came to its twilight
only the dawn would restore the daffodil,
which had clammed up and was only
to open when the rains came.

Alighting softly on the daffodil the butterfly
that had returned to the daffodil
was satiated and murmured thanks.
There was a bond as the daffodil became unfurled
as the sun shone upon her.
All summer they sat and painted her.

They even thought of a salad
within which to eat her.
They discussed her at length when she
was on her way out getting old, aging and dying
as her time came to be reborn next spring
to reclaim her glory and greet us all
in her magical, mysterious, salutations.

Curven Howell

THE HUNTERS

Rummaging through the dark forest, the hungers thump as one.
Small fragile plants are trodden on and bushes pushed out of the way
in search of fresh blood.
Anger deep in the furrows of these burly men with heavy guns.
As the seconds tick by their hate and rage multiply sinking into the
pits of their souls.
Every movement is purposeful, every expression is cold and each
breath is methodically hard and fast.
Every pore on every body is covered with sweat and anger.
Then in one quick glance followed a second later by a click the anger
is dissolved as a fox's death provides a smile to these hunters.

Sunil Chandarana

SPOILED SUNSET

The golden glow towards the west
so slowly fades, with darker streaks
of pale, pale cloud against the rosy sky
resembling the eyebrows
of the white-haired, sunburnt shepherd who delights
in weather fair.

Trees just showing bud, are limned
in dark, dark contrast
'gainst the aftermath of setting sun.
But beauty here is stamped into the ground
as man's own contribution can be found
compared, in black, stark straightness,
to the delicately twisted boughs of oak and elm.

Monstrous metal megaliths marching,
tethered, like slaves, by bonds of looping wire,
across a lovely land,
carrying both death and power
and making hideous the beauty of the evening hour.

David Garde

WINTER

Winter is here again.
To a rich man
in the comfort of his home,
winter is a friend
or merely a change of season.
But to a homeless man on the streets
winter must surely
be an enemy,
sent to kill him in his sleep.
The cold and the damp,
which gets worse
at night,
when the moon shines like a lamp
providing nomads and insomniacs light.
Who's to blame for his circumstance -
the system, society,
or himself?
Is he like the politician says, a lazy bum
who would rather live in a slum
and beg for crumbs
instead
of getting a job?
Or is he like the economist says, an unfortunate,
uncontrollable by-product of capitalism?
Or is he that
which
is ignored by us in our busy everyday lives
because he reminds us
that if we don't work our self to the bone and chase money,
we could be in his shoes tomorrow?

Or is he the brother that instead of helping,
we selfishly leave in sorrow,
because we are inherently egotistic and self-obsessed?
Ah, who cares anyway?
It's time to let my pen have a rest.

Jonathan Kofi Poku

THE SEA

Every day the picture changes,
Rough, smooth, we never can tell;
A large, living canvas of water,
With waves that rise and swell.

Things are hidden beneath the depths,
Creatures we've never seen;
Things that we only read about
In books and magazines.

People should treat it with respect,
The power is strong and deadly;
It will strike on the unaware,
The lives it takes end sadly.

The other side is calm and smooth,
With waves lapping gently in;
Children frolic around the edges,
Should they paddle or go for a swim.

Many people try to pollute it,
Chemicals they constantly pump in;
They should understand the consequences,
To the sea and everything within.

The sea has always been our best friend,
It has always kept us safe;
From many marauding invaders,
What would have been our fate?

Janet Gardner

THE SHIRES

See green fields washed with summer sun,
A soft breeze blows and trees are undulating.
Shaded, he sits in silent contemplation; waiting
Now, by the corner gate, the brewer's van.
A man unhinges; impinges; but in good cause.
A pause, as he lets down the tailboard and they
Are led blinking into the sunlight; funlight!
The holiday is here!
Four dapple greys in uniform, await the chance
To be reborn. The air's alive with expectation;
Exploration, and the new adventure.
Quivers of anticipation; halters loosened, exultation!
Trotting first to take a baring, then the others joining -
Haring round the lush enclosure; gone is all equine composure.
Manes a-flying, tails like flags, nothing hinders,
Nothing drags, no restraints; no wooden shafts
No jingling harness; heavy drafts.
A leap, a buck, an agile dance. An elegant resolve to prance.
They canter proudly in a line, and doing so display
A fine regality.

James Merrick

MY MOUNTAIN HOME

I sing of the beauty of my mountain home
Where swallows are diving around my haystacks
The blackbirds are singing of the promise of spring
And the roses are bursting by the bright morning sun

And Rover, my sheepdog, is ready to go
Up the lanes of heather and ferns
The skylark is early - he's up in the sky
His partner is resting in the meadow below

Sweet music is coming from the thorn in white bloom
A greenfinch is singing and the robin so sweet
To live on the mountain
Is like Heaven itself
Where fresh air is a-plenty
And the company your own.

Patrick McCrory

AN OCEAN OF SENSES

To hear the sea sounding its symphony
Touching me deep where no other mortal thing can reach
Rushing, immersing, flowing through me like blood
Gently stroking my hair
Balancing on the tiniest tip of my toenail

The smell, the sight
Igniting all senses
So open, eternal, powerful and free
Guiding my thoughts, my trailing dreams
Trickling down my mind
A waterfall of possibilities

The past, the experience, the wisdom
All put proudly in their place
Locked away, resurfacing over the passing of time
Waves open selected doors, leaking out certain memories
And to create new intentions
The calm hush-hush . . . ssshhhh!
Gently crawling the sand,
The sea and my soul
Embrace, locked hand in hand.

S Grayson

DAYBREAK TO DUSK

As golden streaks of light creep across the sky
And the peaceful calm of dawn is all around,
A faint twittering of demand from trees on high
Hails this new day with ever-increasing sound.

The crescendo of 'dawn chorus' is in full swing
And the world awakes to welcome life on Earth,
Still unknown to it what future hours will bring,
Maybe new love, new hope or perhaps new birth.

As the drowsiness of waking hours revives,
Energy conserved for just another day,
Movements of most people with their busy lives
In memory linger on, some forever stay.

In busy towns the dull drone of traffic sounds
And the twitterings of most fledglings now unheard,
As the work of some wildlife still abounds
The search for food, daily tasks of hungry birds.

The countryside blessed with a language of its own
Busy farmers tend their hungry flocks and herds
Gratitude is then so very quickly shown,
Animals making noises, substituting words.

Children preparing for yet another day
Where their lives subdued, consist of valued work,
Hours of release welcomed, happy then to play,
But from these hours of learning, they should not shirk.

And as we carry on with our daily toil
For the survival of family, come what may,
We must share concern for nature and not spoil
Conditions for food growth needed day by day.

As the light of day returns to night-time hour,
Sweet notes of evensong echo from each bower.

I Grahame

UNTITLED

The colours of a
Perfect world
My world
The clear fresh sky
Lays neatly on the
Lazy sandy beach
Disturbed by the
Clear cool sea
Lapping, trying so effortlessly
Not to create any ripples
I would love to just tip
My toe in the water
But the peaceful trance
Creates tension, the waves
Almost angry that
I would want to touch them
The sun caressing my body
So delicate with its touch
A voice calls me
Be back tomorrow
I whisper, thank you for today.

Rachel Baldwin

RUSTIC SUMMER

The summer is here and the swallows swoop
As the flying ants crowd the sultry air,
In a tower of winged life and death,
O'er Bodgers Wood and the churchyard there.

The daytime's sound fades to the evening's hush,
The cattle lie, tired, below the trees,
Flicking their tails to flight the dreaded clegg
As distant thunder rumbles o'er the leas.

The anxious farmer looks towards the south,
The paddock's bull now looks towards the cows,
To consider his options with glowering eyes,
Then lowers his head and continues to browse.

Now the crops are in and 'tis Harvest Home
The barn's sides bulge and the ricks are tall,
The swallows have gone and the ants are no more,
And the apples picked before the ripe fruit falls.

And lovers walk in the evening's air,
As moths flit and beetles drone o'er the fields,
The farmer looks out o'er his stubbled land,
Well satisfied with the season's yield.

John Whittock

WONDERMENT

We take all for granted as each season comes and goes
Each season has an allotted time as the years disclose
After perhaps a cold winter it is surprising to see
Nature is stirring and putting forth green so fantastically
All is slowly waking up, they hear this special call
Bulbs and seeds revitalised to sprout and give their all
This being the same with trees and plants they herald the spring
As if slowly upon this stage all commence blossoming

Those that appreciate the garden with nature share
The joy and preservation of growth nurtured with due care
Observe many surprising results that eventually arise from the soil
Delighted grows our garden and the fragrance is extolled
Replenishing the tired soil with welcoming ingredients
Watered and weeded all wait patiently and very obedient
At a given time they appear in rows, lines or drills
Climbing either on canes or trailing like the vine

It's a miracle as each season a new beauty unfurls
Like a stage play with many colours and many parts to observe
From spring to winter should there be dulled grey skies
There is always nature to respond for human eyes
Even delightful window boxes or hanging baskets high
Is a work of art by nature and a joy to those that pass by
I adore my cottage garden wherein dwell many flowers
Appreciating the pleasure they give whilst I while away the hours.

R D Hiscoke

MUSIC OF THE NIGHT

How still! The dark flower of countryside
at rest and motionless, like a pool
not rumpled by a single wing
and all the long, quiet breaths of stars
drift down across the grass.
And out of this calm balance comes the rasp
of legs, patient saws calling out for love
slow as the resting heart
the rhythm of languorous lust

I listen. Beneath is yet another voice,
softer in its own pace, different legs
calling a different love
orchestrated moves that blend the notes
of fainter still another song,
another aria of night,
the smallest violin.

Karen Eberhardt Shelton

THE SEASONS

Life is a mixture of snow, sun and rain
But now spring has sprung again
Where flowers blossom in the sun
When brightness once more, overcomes

The trees blossom, with lilac and lime
As the leaves seem to whisper, with rhythm and rhyme
When God once more covers the leaves, on the trees
When autumn cold months start to cease

While squirrels like to run and play
When once winter had its own way
With glooms of mist, and cold snow
Followed by autumn, then spring's shining glow

While gathering bluebells, around the country way
Apple blossom trees start to swing, and sway
Against a gentle breeze, that seems to be whistling
When once the flames of autumn, were once bright, and burning

Now, spring brings the brightness all around
While, tulips bloom once more upon the ground
Showing their fragrance, and different colours
Through the spring's glorious shining hours

Until summer meets the spring, and the swallows sing
To a twittering varying tone, produced on their wing
Till the twilight appears, and through the deep of the night
The nightingales, call, under the pale moonlight

Showing their white beams across their throats
A melody sounds, with their rich, varied, pure, liquid notes
Through the mixtures of the four seasons
Summer nights also bring the pleasure, through God's creation.

Jean P McGovern

THE SEASONS

Halfway, thro' winter and spring,
It is one day cold, the next day not!
Sometimes, it's winter woollies,
Other days, they are too hot!
Winter is still in the offing,
But it's spring you are thinking about,
Daffodils, golden forsythia, blossom
Of almond and cherry, give spring clout!

Before there is time to decide
Which of the seasons we're in,
Summer is on the horizon,
And the quandary begins again!
The truth of the matter seems to be,
Seasons are no longer clear!
So we choose for ourselves the season,
Then it can be summer throughout the year!

Summer, autumn, winter or spring,
Some good days, some bad, in them all,
For me, well - I just adore springtime,
Or do I prefer the fall?
England in spring is fabulous,
I even like winter's snow!
Summertime sun? It's glorious,
But autumn? That's nature's best show!

E M Eagle

ON BRUNTWOOD POND

Swirling mist drifts through the trees, a chill is in the air
White frost covers like a shroud, all the forest bare
A robin with his scarlet breast sits upon a log
The holly bush with berries red, the cold December fog
Fir trees stand against the sky, sprinkled with the snow
Children skating on the pond, hands and faces glow
Snowflakes like confetti fall, gently to the ground
Covering the forest bed, quickly, without a sound
Happily the children play on sledges down the hill
Or skating on the frozen pond behind the village mill
Teatime comes they all disperse into their cosy homes
Toasting muffins on coal fires, eating buttered scones
Fairy lights dance around the branches of the trees
Flashing brightly coloured lights that look like glassy leaves
Snow is falling thick and fast, covering all in sight
There's nothing like a real coal fire on a winter's night.

Pat Bradley

SWINGING INTO SUMMER

Under trees heavy with blossom
Parents shepherd their children
Over the crossing
As traffic cruises uphill
Toward cold cemeteries
And old gypsy encampments
As children wing into summer
Or whirl on rusting carousels.

Paul Wilkins

THE SUNDIAL

I greet the spring
With ivy tongues,
The smooth-chiselled brilliance:
A pretty thing.

Birds weave the air
Above in dull
Leaden showers
Without a care
To the distant sea.
(The black swans
nest in Dawlish.)

Time
Is heard and heard
Again in the house
The clock strikes out its summer rhyme
Uncouth.

Nicola Barnes

THE AFTERMATH: AS SPRING DAWNS

Deep in a hollow the land before dawn lies silent and moist 'cross the
side of the knoll.
A cold north-east wind blows bitter its wrath, through covers of beech,
bending their boughs,
spilling their blood from craggèd bark as it splits and spits in the eyes of
the foe.
Spewing tears of defiance from shivering pores off leaves so silver in
shards of moonlight.
Pools of fresh water in hoof-moulded furrows lie betwixt rain-sodden
clods, hugging the earth,
eluding the howling and writhing of armies of spirits, marching 'cross
moorland in the wake of the wind.
Whose razor-sharp clawing, splinters the branches in dense vegetation
witnessed by no one save pheasant and deer, cowering lifeless
in mulch-covered hovels 'neath blankets of darkness and ghosts of
the past.
Spirits of soldiers, women and children scream from the valley, their
water-logged graveyard,
cries of their misery hover with kestrels suspended on currents of
turbulent air.
Raging and roaring, ripping off roof tops, the wind and his army lay
waste the victims of war.
Like runts in a litter the strongest survive as old father oak casts an eye
o'er his saplings,
quivering, trembling, clinging to hillsides with roots entwined in twisted
formation,
round bones of the innocent, angry and brave.

Meandering slowly, the river below hears nothing save
droplets of water, playing with boatmen, tickling duck-weed
beneath the watch of the silvery moon.

Susan Seward

DANDELION CLOCKS

Dandelion clocks sway gently in the breeze
which ruffles my hair,
once upon a time, I measured time,
the hours
with gentle puffs on its white, bearded head
watching the seeds disperse in lumpy clusters
to continue the cycle of propagation once again.
Life progresses on, in slow, steady marching time
no turning back to those long, slow, sultry
childish days.
We hurtle relentlessly on
vainly struggling to keep abreast of change,
which has become
our daily diet of fear.
The future lies
all unknown
views glimpsed of a far and distant country.

Frances Anne

THE BLACK ORCHID

I feel life stirring within me,
The sun shines on the moist brown earth,
I want to reach up and touch those rays of light,
The days stretch out in languid bliss,

My growth is strong,
My beauty is the majesty of my birth,
The days are long and the nights are cool,
My flower grows stronger,

I am nurtured, the breeze is gentle on my petals,
My beauty is admired, oh how I am blessed,
My cousins grow beside me, what colours these beauties are,
My flower is black, how come?

Am I damned to have this black coat?
I grow distressed, my leaves bend,
These humans come to look at me,
Now I know I am special, I am a black orchid.

Elizabeth Hiddleston

PASSED BEAUTY

Long hair
glorying in
sunlight
traversing
the grand
square
long skirt
billowing
dancing flag
mirroring
coloured
airflow of
urban textures
head angled
towards
Heaven's
Gift

Séamas M Ó Dálaigh

END OF THE SEASON

When the season has finally ended
And the last of the tourists has gone:
When the last of the litter is all swept away
And the covers have all been put on
The rides and the swings and the sideshows,
And the deckchairs are safely stowed;
When the candyfloss kiosks are shuttered
And the donkeys are in their abode;
When the speedboats are all at their moorings
And the pleasure-steamer's in dock;
When you can't buy a crab or a winkle,
Or a stick of lettered-through rock,
Does the castle pull up its drawbridge
And the lighthouse put out its light?
Do the seagulls huddle together
And kiss each other goodnight?
Does the town go to sleep for the winter,
Hibernating to try and keep warm
As the rain and the gales lash the houses
In the teeth of the howling storm?
Then, when the winter is over
And the first tourist knocks on the door,
Do they set off a giant alarm clock
To wake up the town and the shore?

Richard Young

ONE NIGHT

On a cold winter's night
When the sky was grey,
I saw a white fox
Running away,
Its nose was small,
Its fur was thick,
It had a large tail,
In its mouth was a stick.
I looked at the fox,
The fox looked at me,
It came up to the house
And stood under the tree.
Temptation overcame me
To be nearer to this fox,
I went down to the front door
And undid several locks.
When I got outside
The air was clean,
I looked around, but
The fox was nowhere to be seen.
I looked over the hedge,
Wandered off into town,
Almost fell off the bridge
In my worn and torn gown.
I searched over the hills,
Even looked at the mountains,
I crossed the motorway
Near the newly built fountains.
At the end of the night
I was tattered and torn,
So I made my way back
To my own front lawn.

I got into bed
And went straight to sleep,
Woke up in the morning,
I'd had the worst dream.

Rina Ghataora

MORNING BREAKS

Oh! Morning breaks with springtime dew,
A spider's web, spun just for you,
Is this the start of something new,
To feel the breeze that softly blows
And you are loved
For Heaven knows,
And as we stroll on golden beach
Bliss is well within our reach,
So slumber now
And in your dreams
Just imagine
        Shimmering
        Streams!

Brian Akers

A SUNDAY STROLL

I walked today down a quiet country lane
And for the first time in a long time, I felt completely sane.
Far from the madness of rush hour commuters,
The pressure of time and gluttony of computers,
I was awed by the splendour of autumn glory
As nature unfolded her seasonal story.
My eyes captured riches of copper and gold,
Treasures indeed for memory to hold.
As I walked down that lane I felt humble and small,
Like a serf treading timidly through a great palace hall.
The trees lined each side, so royal and tall,
Bedecked with the brilliance of queens for a ball.
Bright red, mellow yellow and emerald green
Perfection in colour, magnificent in scene.
The rustle of leaves was like the swish of silk gowns
And the shafts of sunlight shone like jewels in a crown.
The wind called the tune as the great boughs did sway,
Nonchalantly tossing their gold leaves away.
Soon the last leaf will fall and lie still,
Bare trees will surrender to winter's will.
They will sleep while frost reigns and birds cease to sing
And dream of awakening to the whisper of spring.

Janet Petchey

I HAVE TO SEE SUMMER

I have to see summer once more;
Before the leaves begin to turn,
Ere autumn's colours brightly burn
Amidst the trees, the woodland o'er.

I have to walk the green trimmed lane,
To watch the cornfield's golden frieze
Rippling like water in the breeze,
A bright and shining counterpane.

I must stride out beneath the sky,
Gaze at the apple-laden boughs
Across the lea where cattle browse,
Where hovers still the butterfly.

I must behold the swallows' height,
Hear distant willow warblers pipe,
Savour blackberries, juicy and ripe.
Stay sweet season! Take not to flight!

Evelyn Balmain

THE CEDAR TREE

I overlook them all, elm, ash, willow, lime,
For I have stretched my boughs, heavenwards,
Tall and stately, yet, delicately,
Upward, upward, till it seems that I might flirt and frolic
With the clouds,
And, like my brother trees, I live in constant fear of extinction,
Tall, stately, no bird's nest tangle in my hair,
Tall, stately - 'Why,' folk say, 'just look at its magnificence,
So very tall and stately.'
Pure bred I am, my lineage is ancient and has no flaw,
I am mentioned in historic tomes;
I am revered by gentle lovers who, fused together ecstatically,
Bathe in the scent of my rich perfume;
I have been to war, in weaponry,
So firm, yet so supple am I,
I am the mighty cedar.

L Park